FIPS PUB 180-4

FEDERAL INFORMATION PROCESSING STANDARDS
PUBLICATION

Secure Hash Standard (SHS)

CATEGORY: COMPUTER SECURITY   SUBCATEGORY: CRYPTOGRAPHY

Information Technology Laboratory
National Institute of Standards and Technology
Gaithersburg, MD 20899-8900

March 2012

U.S. Department of Commerce
John Bryson, Secretary

National Institute of Standards and Technology
Patrick Gallagher, Under Secretary for Standards and Technology and Director

FOREWORD

The Federal Information Processing Standards Publication Series of the National Institute of Standards and Technology (NIST) is the official series of publications relating to standards and guidelines adopted and promulgated under the provisions of the Federal Information Security Management Act (FISMA) of 2002.

Comments concerning FIPS publications are welcomed and should be addressed to the Director, Information Technology Laboratory, National Institute of Standards and Technology, 100 Bureau Drive, Stop 8900, Gaithersburg, MD 20899-8900.

Charles H. Romine, Director
Information Technology Laboratory

Abstract

This standard specifies hash algorithms that can be used to generate digests of messages. The digests are used to detect whether messages have been changed since the digests were generated.

Key words: computer security, cryptography, message digest, hash function, hash algorithm, Federal Information Processing Standards, Secure Hash Standard.

**Federal Information
Processing Standards Publication 180-4**

March 2012

Announcing the

SECURE HASH STANDARD

Federal Information Processing Standards Publications (FIPS PUBS) are issued by the National Institute of Standards and Technology (NIST) after approval by the Secretary of Commerce pursuant to Section 5131 of the Information Technology Management Reform Act of 1996 (Public Law 104-106), and the Computer Security Act of 1987 (Public Law 100-235).

1. **Name of Standard**: Secure Hash Standard (SHS) (FIPS PUB 180-4).

2. **Category of Standard**: Computer Security Standard, Cryptography.

3. **Explanation**: This Standard specifies secure hash algorithms - SHA-1, SHA-224, SHA-256, SHA-384, SHA-512, SHA-512/224 and SHA-512/256 - for computing a condensed representation of electronic data (message). When a message of any length less than 2^{64} bits (for SHA-1, SHA-224 and SHA-256) or less than 2^{128} bits (for SHA-384, SHA-512, SHA-512/224 and SHA-512/256) is input to a hash algorithm, the result is an output called a message digest. The message digests range in length from 160 to 512 bits, depending on the algorithm. Secure hash algorithms are typically used with other cryptographic algorithms, such as digital signature algorithms and keyed-hash message authentication codes, or in the generation of random numbers (bits).

The hash algorithms specified in this Standard are called secure because, for a given algorithm, it is computationally infeasible 1) to find a message that corresponds to a given message digest, or 2) to find two different messages that produce the same message digest. Any change to a message will, with a very high probability, result in a different message digest. This will result in a verification failure when the secure hash algorithm is used with a digital signature algorithm or a keyed-hash message authentication algorithm.

This Standard supersedes FIPS 180-3 [FIPS 180-3].

4. **Approving Authority**: Secretary of Commerce.

5. **Maintenance Agency**: U.S. Department of Commerce, National Institute of Standards and Technology (NIST), Information Technology Laboratory (ITL).

6. Applicability: This Standard is applicable to all Federal departments and agencies for the protection of sensitive unclassified information that is not subject to Title 10 United States Code Section 2315 (10 USC 2315) and that is not within a national security system as defined in Title 44 United States Code Section 3502(2) (44 USC 3502(2)). This standard shall be implemented whenever a secure hash algorithm is required for Federal applications, including use by other cryptographic algorithms and protocols. The adoption and use of this Standard is available to private and commercial organizations.

7. Specifications: Federal Information Processing Standard (FIPS) 180-4, Secure Hash Standard (SHS) (affixed).

8. Implementations: The secure hash algorithms specified herein may be implemented in software, firmware, hardware or any combination thereof. Only algorithm implementations that are validated by NIST will be considered as complying with this standard. Information about the validation program can be obtained at http://csrc.nist.gov/groups/STM/index.html.

9. Implementation Schedule: Guidance regarding the testing and validation to FIPS 180-4 and its relationship to FIPS 140-2 can be found in IG 1.10 of the Implementation Guidance for FIPS PUB 140-2 and the Cryptographic Module Validation Program at http://csrc.nist.gov/groups/STM/cmvp/index.html.

10. Patents: Implementations of the secure hash algorithms in this standard may be covered by U.S. or foreign patents.

11. Export Control: Certain cryptographic devices and technical data regarding them are subject to Federal export controls. Exports of cryptographic modules implementing this standard and technical data regarding them must comply with these Federal regulations and be licensed by the Bureau of Export Administration of the U.S. Department of Commerce. Information about export regulations is available at: http://www.bis.doc.gov/index.htm.

12. Qualifications: While it is the intent of this Standard to specify general security requirements for generating a message digest, conformance to this Standard does not assure that a particular implementation is secure. The responsible authority in each agency or department shall assure that an overall implementation provides an acceptable level of security. This Standard will be reviewed every five years in order to assess its adequacy.

13. Waiver Procedure: The Federal Information Security Management Act (FISMA) does not allow for waivers to Federal Information Processing Standards (FIPS) that are made mandatory by the Secretary of Commerce.

14. Where to Obtain Copies of the Standard: This publication is available electronically by accessing http://csrc.nist.gov/publications/. Other computer security publications are available at the same web site.

**Federal Information
Processing Standards Publication 180-4**

Specifications for the

SECURE HASH STANDARD

Table of Contents

1.	**INTRODUCTION**	**3**
2.	**DEFINITIONS**	**4**
	2.1 GLOSSARY OF TERMS AND ACRONYMS	4
	2.2 ALGORITHM PARAMETERS, SYMBOLS, AND TERMS	4
	2.2.1 *Parameters*	*4*
	2.2.2 *Symbols and Operations*	*5*
3.	**NOTATION AND CONVENTIONS**	**7**
	3.1 BIT STRINGS AND INTEGERS	7
	3.2 OPERATIONS ON WORDS	8
4.	**FUNCTIONS AND CONSTANTS**	**10**
	4.1 FUNCTIONS	10
	4.1.1 *SHA-1 Functions*	*10*
	4.1.2 *SHA-224 and SHA-256 Functions*	*10*
	4.1.3 *SHA-384, SHA-512, SHA-512/224 and SHA-512/256 Functions* ...	*11*
	4.2 CONSTANTS	11
	4.2.1 *SHA-1 Constants*	*11*
	4.2.2 *SHA-224 and SHA-256 Constants*	*11*
	4.2.3 *SHA-384, SHA-512, SHA-512/224 and SHA-512/256 Constants* ...	*12*
5.	**PREPROCESSING**	**13**
	5.1 PADDING THE MESSAGE	13
	5.1.1 *SHA-1, SHA-224 and SHA-256*	*13*
	5.1.2 *SHA-384, SHA-512, SHA-512/224 and SHA-512/256*	*13*
	5.2 PARSING THE MESSAGE	14
	5.2.1 *SHA-1, SHA-224 and SHA-256*	*14*
	5.2.2 *SHA-384, SHA-512, SHA-512/224 and SHA-512/256*	*14*
	5.3 SETTING THE INITIAL HASH VALUE ($H^{(0)}$)	14
	5.3.1 *SHA-1*	*14*
	5.3.2 *SHA-224*	*14*
	5.3.3 *SHA-256*	*15*
	5.3.4 *SHA-384*	*15*
	5.3.5 *SHA-512*	*15*
	5.3.6 *SHA-512/t*	*16*
	5.3.6.1 SHA-512/224	17
	5.3.6.2 SHA-512/256	17
6.	**SECURE HASH ALGORITHMS**	**18**
	6.1 SHA-1	18

      6.1.1   SHA-1 Preprocessing...*18*
      6.1.2   SHA-1 Hash Computation *18*
      6.1.3   Alternate Method for Computing a SHA-1 Message Digest.....................*20*
6.2   SHA-256 21
      6.2.1   SHA-256 Preprocessing..*22*
      6.2.2   SHA-256 Hash Computation *22*
6.3   SHA-224 23
6.4   SHA-512 24
      6.4.1   SHA-512 Preprocessing..*24*
      6.4.2   SHA-512 Hash Computation *24*
6.5   SHA-384 26
6.6   SHA-512/224 26
6.7   SHA-512/256 26

7.   **TRUNCATION OF A MESSAGE DIGEST** **27**

APPENDIX A: ADDITIONAL INFORMATION **28**
A.1   SECURITY OF THE SECURE HASH ALGORITHMS 28
A.2   IMPLEMENTATION NOTES 28
A.3   OBJECT IDENTIFIERS 28

APPENDIX B: REFERENCES **29**

APPENDIX C: TECHNICAL CHANGES FROM FIPS 180-3 ....**30**

1. INTRODUCTION

This Standard specifies secure hash algorithms, SHA-1, SHA-224, SHA-256, SHA-384, SHA-512, SHA-512/224 and SHA-512/256. All of the algorithms are iterative, one-way hash functions that can process a message to produce a condensed representation called a *message digest*. These algorithms enable the determination of a message's integrity: any change to the message will, with a very high probability, result in a different message digest. This property is useful in the generation and verification of digital signatures and message authentication codes, and in the generation of random numbers or bits.

Each algorithm can be described in two stages: preprocessing and hash computation. Preprocessing involves padding a message, parsing the padded message into m-bit blocks, and setting initialization values to be used in the hash computation. The hash computation generates a *message schedule* from the padded message and uses that schedule, along with functions, constants, and word operations to iteratively generate a series of hash values. The final hash value generated by the hash computation is used to determine the message digest.

The algorithms differ most significantly in the security strengths that are provided for the data being hashed. The security strengths of these hash functions and the system as a whole when each of them is used with other cryptographic algorithms, such as digital signature algorithms and keyed-hash message authentication codes, can be found in [SP 800-57] and [SP 800-107].

Additionally, the algorithms differ in terms of the size of the blocks and words of data that are used during hashing or message digest sizes. Figure 1 presents the basic properties of these hash algorithms.

Algorithm	Message Size (bits)	Block Size (bits)	Word Size (bits)	Message Digest Size (bits)
SHA-1	$< 2^{64}$	512	32	160
SHA-224	$< 2^{64}$	512	32	224
SHA-256	$< 2^{64}$	512	32	256
SHA-384	$< 2^{128}$	1024	64	384
SHA-512	$< 2^{128}$	1024	64	512
SHA-512/224	$< 2^{128}$	1024	64	224
SHA-512/256	$< 2^{128}$	1024	64	256

Figure 1: Secure Hash Algorithm Properties

2. DEFINITIONS

2.1 Glossary of Terms and Acronyms

Bit	A binary digit having a value of 0 or 1.
Byte	A group of eight bits.
FIPS	Federal Information Processing Standard.
NIST	National Institute of Standards and Technology.
SHA	Secure Hash Algorithm.
SP	Special Publication
Word	A group of either 32 bits (4 bytes) or 64 bits (8 bytes), depending on the secure hash algorithm.

2.2 Algorithm Parameters, Symbols, and Terms

2.2.1 Parameters

The following parameters are used in the secure hash algorithm specifications in this Standard.

$a, b, c, ..., h$	Working variables that are the w-bit words used in the computation of the hash values, $H^{(i)}$.
$H^{(i)}$	The ith hash value. $H^{(0)}$ is the *initial* hash value; $H^{(N)}$ is the *final* hash value and is used to determine the message digest.
$H_j^{(i)}$	The jth word of the ith hash value, where $H_0^{(i)}$ is the left-most word of hash value i.
K_t	Constant value to be used for the iteration t of the hash computation.
k	Number of zeroes appended to a message during the padding step.
ℓ	Length of the message, M, in bits.
m	Number of bits in a message block, $M^{(i)}$.
M	Message to be hashed.

$M^{(i)}$	Message block i, with a size of m bits.
$M_j^{(i)}$	The jth word of the ith message block, where $M_0^{(i)}$ is the left-most word of message block i.
n	Number of bits to be rotated or shifted when a word is operated upon.
N	Number of blocks in the padded message.
T	Temporary w-bit word used in the hash computation.
w	Number of bits in a word.
W_t	The tth w-bit word of the message schedule.

2.2.2 Symbols and Operations

The following symbols are used in the secure hash algorithm specifications; each operates on w-bit words.

$\wedge$	Bitwise AND operation.
$\vee$	Bitwise OR ("inclusive-OR") operation.
$\oplus$	Bitwise XOR ("exclusive-OR") operation.
$\neg$	Bitwise complement operation.
$+$	Addition modulo 2^w.
$<<$	Left-shift operation, where $x << n$ is obtained by discarding the left-most n bits of the word x and then padding the result with n zeroes on the right.
$>>$	Right-shift operation, where $x >> n$ is obtained by discarding the right-most n bits of the word x and then padding the result with n zeroes on the left.

The following operations are used in the secure hash algorithm specifications:

$ROTL^n(x)$	The *rotate left* (circular left shift) operation, where x is a w-bit word and n is an integer with $0 \leq n < w$, is defined by $ROTL^n(x) = (x << n) \vee (x >> w - n)$.
$ROTR^n(x)$	The *rotate right* (circular right shift) operation, where x is a w-bit word and n is an integer with $0 \leq n < w$, is defined by $ROTR^n(x) = (x >> n) \vee (x << w - n)$.

SHR^n(x)   The *right shift* operation, where x is a w-bit word and n is an integer with $0 \leq n < w$, is defined by $SHR^n(x) = x \gg n$.

3.   NOTATION AND CONVENTIONS

3.1   Bit Strings and Integers

The following terminology related to bit strings and integers will be used.

1. A *hex digit* is an element of the set $\{0, 1, ..., 9, a, ..., f\}$. A hex digit is the representation of a 4-bit string. For example, the hex digit "7" represents the 4-bit string "0111", and the hex digit "a" represents the 4-bit string "1010".

2. A *word* is a w-bit string that may be represented as a sequence of hex digits. To convert a word to hex digits, each 4-bit string is converted to its hex digit equivalent, as described in (1) above. For example, the 32-bit string

    ```
    1010 0001 0000 0011 1111 1110 0010 0011
    ```

    can be expressed as "a103fe23", and the 64-bit string

    ```
    1010 0001 0000 0011 1111 1110 0010 0011
    0011 0010 1110 1111 0011 0000 0001 1010
    ```

    can be expressed as "a103fe2332ef301a".

    Throughout this specification, the "big-endian" convention is used when expressing both 32- and 64-bit words, so that within each word, the most significant bit is stored in the left-most bit position.

3. An *integer* may be represented as a word or pair of words. A word representation of the message length, ℓ, in bits, is required for the padding techniques of Sec. 5.1.

    An integer between 0 and 2^{32}-1 *inclusive* may be represented as a 32-bit word. The least significant four bits of the integer are represented by the right-most hex digit of the word representation. For example, the integer $291 = 2^8 + 2^5 + 2^1 + 2^0 = 256+32+2+1$ is represented by the hex word "00000123".

    The same holds true for an integer between 0 and 2^{64}-1 *inclusive*, which may be represented as a 64-bit word.

    If Z is an integer, $0 \leq Z < 2^{64}$, then $Z = 2^{32}X + Y$, where $0 \leq X < 2^{32}$ and $0 \leq Y < 2^{32}$. Since X and Y can be represented as 32-bit words x and y, respectively, the integer Z can be represented as the pair of words (x, y). This property is used for SHA-1, SHA-224 and SHA-256.

If Z is an integer, $0 \leq Z < 2^{128}$, then $Z = 2^{64}X + Y$, where $0 \leq X < 2^{64}$ and $0 \leq Y < 2^{64}$. Since X and Y can be represented as 64-bit words x and y, respectively, the integer Z can be represented as the pair of words (x, y). This property is used for SHA-384, SHA-512, SHA-512/224 and SHA-512/256.

4. For the secure hash algorithms, the size of the *message block* - m bits - depends on the algorithm.

   a) For **SHA-1, SHA-224** and **SHA-256**, each message block has **512 bits**, which are represented as a sequence of sixteen **32-bit words**.

   b) For **SHA-384, SHA-512, SHA-512/224** and **SHA-512/256** each message block has **1024 bits**, which are represented as a sequence of sixteen **64-bit words**.

3.2 Operations on Words

The following operations are applied to w-bit words in all five secure hash algorithms. SHA-1, SHA-224 and SHA-256 operate on 32-bit words (w=32), and SHA-384, SHA-512, SHA-512/224 and SHA-512/256 operate on 64-bit words (w=64).

1. Bitwise *logical* word operations: $\wedge$, $\vee$, $\oplus$, and $\neg$ (see Sec. 2.2.2).

2. Addition modulo 2^w.

   The operation $x + y$ is defined as follows. The words x and y represent integers X and Y, where $0 \leq X < 2^w$ and $0 \leq Y < 2^w$. For positive integers U and V, let $U \bmod V$ be the remainder upon dividing U by V. Compute

   $$Z = (X + Y) \bmod 2^w.$$

   Then $0 \leq Z < 2^w$. Convert the integer Z to a word, z, and define $z = x + y$.

3. The *right shift* operation $SHR^n(x)$, where x is a w-bit word and n is an integer with $0 \leq n < w$, is defined by

   $$SHR^n(x) = x >> n.$$

   This operation is used in the SHA-224, SHA-256, SHA-384, SHA-512, SHA-512/224 and SHA-512/256 algorithms.

4. The *rotate right* (circular right shift) operation $ROTR^n(x)$, where x is a w-bit word and n is an integer with $0 \leq n < w$, is defined by

   $$ROTR^n(x) = (x >> n) \vee (x << w - n).$$

8

Thus, $ROTR^n(x)$ is equivalent to a circular shift (rotation) of x by n positions to the right.

This operation is used by the SHA-224, SHA-256, SHA-384, SHA-512, SHA-512/224 and SHA-512/256 algorithms.

5. The *rotate left* (circular left shift) operation, $\boldsymbol{ROTL^n(x)}$, where x is a w-bit word and n is an integer with $0 \le n < w$, is defined by

$$ROTL^n(x) = (x << n) \lor (x >> w - n).$$

Thus, $ROTL^n(x)$ is equivalent to a circular shift (rotation) of x by n positions to the left.

This operation is used only in the SHA-1 algorithm.

6. Note the following equivalence relationships, where w is fixed in each relationship:

$$ROTL^n(x) \approx ROTR^{w-n}(x)$$

$$ROTR^n(x) \approx ROTL^{w-n}(x)$$

4. FUNCTIONS AND CONSTANTS

4.1 Functions

This section defines the functions that are used by each of the algorithms. Although the SHA-224, SHA-256, SHA-384,SHA-512, SHA-512/224 and SHA-512/256 algorithms all use similar functions, their descriptions are separated into sections for SHA-224 and SHA-256 (Sec. 4.1.2) and for SHA-384, SHA-512, SHA-512/224 and SHA-512/256 (Sec. 4.1.3), since the input and output for these functions are words of different sizes. Each of the algorithms include $Ch(x, y, z)$ and $Maj(x, y, z)$ functions; the exclusive-OR operation ($\oplus$) in these functions may be replaced by a bitwise OR operation ($\vee$) and produce identical results.

4.1.1 SHA-1 Functions

SHA-1 uses a sequence of logical functions, $f_0, f_1, \ldots, f_{79}$. Each function f_t, where $0 \leq t < 79$, operates on three 32-bit words, x, y, and z, and produces a 32-bit word as output. The function $f_t(x, y, z)$ is defined as follows:

$$f_t(x, y, z) = \begin{cases} Ch(x, y, z) = (x \wedge y) \oplus (\neg x \wedge z) & 0 \leq t \leq 19 \\ Parity(x, y, z) = x \oplus y \oplus z & 20 \leq t \leq 39 \\ Maj(x, y, z) = (x \wedge y) \oplus (x \wedge z) \oplus (y \wedge z) & 40 \leq t \leq 59 \\ Parity(x, y, z) = x \oplus y \oplus z & 60 \leq t \leq 79. \end{cases} \tag{4.1}$$

4.1.2 SHA-224 and SHA-256 Functions

SHA-224 and SHA-256 both use six logical functions, where *each function operates on 32-bit words*, which are represented as x, y, and z. The result of each function is a new 32-bit word.

$$Ch(x, y, z) = (x \wedge y) \oplus (\neg x \wedge z) \tag{4.2}$$

$$Maj(x, y, z) = (x \wedge y) \oplus (x \wedge z) \oplus (y \wedge z) \tag{4.3}$$

$$\Sigma_0^{\{256\}}(x) = ROTR^2(x) \oplus ROTR^{13}(x) \oplus ROTR^{22}(x) \tag{4.4}$$

$$\Sigma_1^{\{256\}}(x) = ROTR^6(x) \oplus ROTR^{11}(x) \oplus ROTR^{25}(x) \tag{4.5}$$

$$\sigma_0^{\{256\}}(x) = ROTR^7(x) \oplus ROTR^{18}(x) \oplus SHR^3(x) \tag{4.6}$$

$$\sigma_1^{\{256\}}(x) = ROTR^{17}(x) \oplus ROTR^{19}(x) \oplus SHR^{10}(x) \tag{4.7}$$

10

4.1.3 SHA-384, SHA-512, SHA-512/224 and SHA-512/256 Functions

SHA-384, SHA-512, SHA-512/224 and SHA-512/256 use six logical functions, where *each function operates on 64-bit words*, which are represented as x, y, and z. The result of each function is a new 64-bit word.

$$Ch(x,y,z) = (x \wedge y) \oplus (\neg x \wedge z) \tag{4.8}$$

$$Maj(x,y,z) = (x \wedge y) \oplus (x \wedge z) \oplus (y \wedge z) \tag{4.9}$$

$$\sum\nolimits_{0}^{\{512\}}(x) = ROTR^{28}(x) \oplus ROTR^{34}(x) \oplus ROTR^{39}(x) \tag{4.10}$$

$$\sum\nolimits_{1}^{\{512\}}(x) = ROTR^{14}(x) \oplus ROTR^{18}(x) \oplus ROTR^{41}(x) \tag{4.11}$$

$$\sigma_{0}^{\{512\}}(x) = ROTR^{1}(x) \oplus ROTR^{8}(x) \oplus SHR^{7}(x) \tag{4.12}$$

$$\sigma_{1}^{\{512\}}(x) = ROTR^{19}(x) \oplus ROTR^{61}(x) \oplus SHR^{6}(x) \tag{4.13}$$

4.2   Constants

4.2.1 SHA-1 Constants

SHA-1 uses a sequence of eighty constant 32-bit words, K_0, K_1,..., K_{79}, which are given by

$$K_t = \begin{cases} \text{5a827999} & 0 \leq t \leq 19 \\ \text{6ed9eba1} & 20 \leq t \leq 39 \\ \text{8f1bbcdc} & 40 \leq t \leq 59 \\ \text{ca62c1d6} & 60 \leq t \leq 79 \end{cases} \tag{4.14}$$

4.2.2 SHA-224 and SHA-256 Constants

SHA-224 and SHA-256 use the same sequence of sixty-four constant 32-bit words, $K_0^{\{256\}}$, $K_1^{\{256\}}$,..., $K_{63}^{\{256\}}$. These words represent the first thirty-two bits of the fractional parts of the cube roots of the first sixty-four prime numbers. In hex, these constant words are (from left to right)

```
428a2f98 71374491 b5c0fbcf e9b5dba5 3956c25b 59f111f1 923f82a4 ab1c5ed5
d807aa98 12835b01 243185be 550c7dc3 72be5d74 80deb1fe 9bdc06a7 c19bf174
e49b69c1 efbe4786 0fc19dc6 240ca1cc 2de92c6f 4a7484aa 5cb0a9dc 76f988da
983e5152 a831c66d b00327c8 bf597fc7 c6e00bf3 d5a79147 06ca6351 14292967
27b70a85 2e1b2138 4d2c6dfc 53380d13 650a7354 766a0abb 81c2c92e 92722c85
a2bfe8a1 a81a664b c24b8b70 c76c51a3 d192e819 d6990624 f40e3585 106aa070
19a4c116 1e376c08 2748774c 34b0bcb5 391c0cb3 4ed8aa4a 5b9cca4f 682e6ff3
748f82ee 78a5636f 84c87814 8cc70208 90befffa a4506ceb bef9a3f7 c67178f2
```

4.2.3 SHA-384, SHA-512, SHA-512/224 and SHA-512/256 Constants

SHA-384, SHA-512, SHA-512/224 and SHA-512/256 use the same sequence of eighty constant 64-bit words, $K_0^{\{512\}}, K_1^{\{512\}},\ldots,K_{79}^{\{512\}}$. These words represent the first sixty-four bits of the fractional parts of the cube roots of the first eighty prime numbers. In hex, these constant words are (from left to right)

```
428a2f98d728ae22  7137449123ef65cd  b5c0fbcfec4d3b2f  e9b5dba58189dbbc
3956c25bf348b538  59f111f1b605d019  923f82a4af194f9b  ab1c5ed5da6d8118
d807aa98a3030242  12835b0145706fbe  243185be4ee4b28c  550c7dc3d5ffb4e2
72be5d74f27b896f  80deb1fe3b1696b1  9bdc06a725c71235  c19bf174cf692694
e49b69c19ef14ad2  efbe4786384f25e3  0fc19dc68b8cd5b5  240ca1cc77ac9c65
2de92c6f592b0275  4a7484aa6ea6e483  5cb0a9dcbd41fbd4  76f988da831153b5
983e5152ee66dfab  a831c66d2db43210  b00327c898fb213f  bf597fc7beef0ee4
c6e00bf33da88fc2  d5a79147930aa725  06ca6351e003826f  142929670a0e6e70
27b70a8546d22ffc  2e1b21385c26c926  4d2c6dfc5ac42aed  53380d139d95b3df
650a73548baf63de  766a0abb3c77b2a8  81c2c92e47edaee6  92722c851482353b
a2bfe8a14cf10364  a81a664bbc423001  c24b8b70d0f89791  c76c51a30654be30
d192e819d6ef5218  d69906245565a910  f40e35855771202a  106aa07032bbd1b8
19a4c116b8d2d0c8  1e376c085141ab53  2748774cdf8eeb99  34b0bcb5e19b48a8
391c0cb3c5c95a63  4ed8aa4ae3418acb  5b9cca4f7763e373  682e6ff3d6b2b8a3
748f82ee5defb2fc  78a5636f43172f60  84c87814a1f0ab72  8cc702081a6439ec
90befffa23631e28  a4506cebde82bde9  bef9a3f7b2c67915  c67178f2e372532b
ca273eceea26619c  d186b8c721c0c207  eada7dd6cde0eb1e  f57d4f7fee6ed178
06f067aa72176fba  0a637dc5a2c898a6  113f9804bef90dae  1b710b35131c471b
28db77f523047d84  32caab7b40c72493  3c9ebe0a15c9bebc  431d67c49c100d4c
4cc5d4becb3e42b6  597f299cfc657e2a  5fcb6fab3ad6faec  6c44198c4a475817
```

5.   PREPROCESSING

Preprocessing consists of three steps: padding the message, M (Sec. 5.1), parsing the message into message blocks (Sec. 5.2), and setting the initial hash value, $H^{(0)}$ (Sec. 5.3).

5.1   Padding the Message

The purpose of this padding is to ensure that the padded message is a multiple of 512 or 1024 bits, depending on the algorithm. Padding can be inserted before hash computation begins   on a message, or at any other time during the hash computation prior to processing the block(s) that will contain the padding.

5.1.1   SHA-1, SHA-224 and SHA-256

Suppose that the length of the message, M, is ℓ bits. Append the bit "1" to the end of the message, followed by k zero bits, where k is the smallest, non-negative solution to the equation $\ell + 1 + k \equiv 448 \bmod 512$. Then append the 64-bit block that is equal to the number ℓ expressed using a binary representation. For example, the (8-bit ASCII) message "**abc**" has length $8 \times 3 = 24$, so the message is padded with a one bit, then $448 - (24 + 1) = 423$ zero bits, and then the message length, to become the 512-bit padded message

$$\underbrace{01100001}_{\text{“a”}} \quad \underbrace{01100010}_{\text{“b”}} \quad \underbrace{01100011}_{\text{“c”}} \quad 1 \quad \overbrace{00...00}^{423} \quad \underbrace{\overbrace{00...011000}^{64}}_{\ell = 24}$$

The length of the padded message should now be a multiple of 512 bits.

5.1.2   SHA-384, SHA-512, SHA-512/224 and SHA-512/256

Suppose the length of the message M, in bits, is ℓ bits. Append the bit "1" to the end of the message, followed by k zero bits, where k is the smallest non-negative solution to the equation $\ell + 1 + k \equiv 896 \bmod 1024$. Then append the 128-bit block that is equal to the number ℓ expressed using a binary representation. For example, the (8-bit ASCII) message "**abc**" has length $8 \times 3 = 24$, so the message is padded with a one bit, then $896 - (24 + 1) = 871$ zero bits, and then the message length, to become the 1024-bit padded message

$$\underbrace{01100001}_{\text{“a”}} \quad \underbrace{01100010}_{\text{“b”}} \quad \underbrace{01100011}_{\text{“c”}} \quad 1 \quad \overbrace{00...00}^{871} \quad \underbrace{\overbrace{00...011000}^{128}}_{\ell = 24}$$

The length of the padded message should now be a multiple of 1024 bits.

5.2   Parsing the Message

The message and its padding must be parsed into N m-bit blocks.

5.2.1   SHA-1, SHA-224 and SHA-256

For SHA-1, SHA-224 and SHA-256, the message and its padding are parsed into N 512-bit blocks, $M^{(1)}, M^{(2)},\ldots, M^{(N)}$. Since the 512 bits of the input block may be expressed as sixteen 32-bit words, the first 32 bits of message block i are denoted $M_0^{(i)}$, the next 32 bits are $M_1^{(i)}$, and so on up to $M_{15}^{(i)}$.

5.2.2   SHA-384, SHA-512, SHA-512/224 and SHA-512/256

For SHA-384, SHA-512, SHA-512/224 and SHA-512/256, the message and its padding are parsed into N 1024-bit blocks, $M^{(1)}, M^{(2)},\ldots, M^{(N)}$. Since the 1024 bits of the input block may be expressed as sixteen 64-bit words, the first 64 bits of message block i are denoted $M_0^{(i)}$, the next 64 bits are $M_1^{(i)}$, and so on up to $M_{15}^{(i)}$.

5.3   Setting the Initial Hash Value ($H^{(0)}$)

Before hash computation begins for each of the secure hash algorithms, the initial hash value, $H^{(0)}$, must be set. The size and number of words in $H^{(0)}$ depends on the message digest size.

5.3.1   SHA-1

For SHA-1, the initial hash value, $H^{(0)}$, shall consist of the following five 32-bit words, in hex:

$$
\begin{aligned}
H_0^{(0)} &= \text{67452301} \\
H_1^{(0)} &= \text{efcdab89} \\
H_2^{(0)} &= \text{98badcfe} \\
H_3^{(0)} &= \text{10325476} \\
H_4^{(0)} &= \text{c3d2e1f0}
\end{aligned}
$$

5.3.2   SHA-224

For SHA-224, the initial hash value, $H^{(0)}$, shall consist of the following eight 32-bit words, in hex:

$$
\begin{aligned}
H_0^{(0)} &= \text{c1059ed8} \\
H_1^{(0)} &= \text{367cd507} \\
H_2^{(0)} &= \text{3070dd17} \\
H_3^{(0)} &= \text{f70e5939} \\
H_4^{(0)} &= \text{ffc00b31} \\
H_5^{(0)} &= \text{68581511} \\
H_6^{(0)} &= \text{64f98fa7}
\end{aligned}
$$

14

$$H_7^{(0)} = \texttt{befa4fa4}$$

5.3.3 SHA-256

For SHA-256, the initial hash value, $H^{(0)}$, shall consist of the following eight 32-bit words, in hex:

$$H_0^{(0)} = \texttt{6a09e667}$$
$$H_1^{(0)} = \texttt{bb67ae85}$$
$$H_2^{(0)} = \texttt{3c6ef372}$$
$$H_3^{(0)} = \texttt{a54ff53a}$$
$$H_4^{(0)} = \texttt{510e527f}$$
$$H_5^{(0)} = \texttt{9b05688c}$$
$$H_6^{(0)} = \texttt{1f83d9ab}$$
$$H_7^{(0)} = \texttt{5be0cd19}$$

These words were obtained by taking the first thirty-two bits of the fractional parts of the square roots of the first eight prime numbers.

5.3.4 SHA-384

For SHA-384, the initial hash value, $H^{(0)}$, shall consist of the following eight 64-bit words, in hex:

$$H_0^{(0)} = \texttt{cbbb9d5dc1059ed8}$$
$$H_1^{(0)} = \texttt{629a292a367cd507}$$
$$H_2^{(0)} = \texttt{9159015a3070dd17}$$
$$H_3^{(0)} = \texttt{152fecd8f70e5939}$$
$$H_4^{(0)} = \texttt{67332667ffc00b31}$$
$$H_5^{(0)} = \texttt{8eb44a8768581511}$$
$$H_6^{(0)} = \texttt{db0c2e0d64f98fa7}$$
$$H_7^{(0)} = \texttt{47b5481dbefa4fa4}$$

These words were obtained by taking the first sixty-four bits of the fractional parts of the square roots of the ninth through sixteenth prime numbers.

5.3.5 SHA-512

For SHA-512, the initial hash value, $H^{(0)}$, shall consist of the following eight 64-bit words, in hex:

$$H_0^{(0)} = \texttt{6a09e667f3bcc908}$$
$$H_1^{(0)} = \texttt{bb67ae8584caa73b}$$

$$H_2^{(0)} = \text{3c6ef372fe94f82b}$$
$$H_3^{(0)} = \text{a54ff53a5f1d36f1}$$
$$H_4^{(0)} = \text{510e527fade682d1}$$
$$H_5^{(0)} = \text{9b05688c2b3e6c1f}$$
$$H_6^{(0)} = \text{1f83d9abfb41bd6b}$$
$$H_7^{(0)} = \text{5be0cd19137e2179}$$

These words were obtained by taking the first sixty-four bits of the fractional parts of the square roots of the first eight prime numbers.

5.3.6   SHA-512/t

"SHA-512/t" is the general name for a t-bit hash function based on SHA-512 whose output is truncated to t bits. Each hash function requires a distinct initial hash value. This section provides a procedure for determining the initial value for SHA-512/t for a given value of t.

For SHA-512/t, t is any positive integer without a leading zero such that $t < 512$, and t is not 384. For example: t is 256, but not 0256, and "SHA-512/t" is "SHA-512/256" (an 11 character long ASCII string), which is equivalent to 53 48 41 2D 35 31 32 2F 32 35 36 in hexadecimal.

The initial hash value for SHA-512/t, for a given value of t, shall be generated by the *SHA-512/t IV Generation Function* below.

SHA-512/t IV Generation Function

(begin:)

Denote $H^{(0)'}$ to be the initial hash value of SHA-512 as specified in Section 5.3.5 above.

Denote $H^{(0)''}$ to be the initial hash value computed below.

$H^{(0)}$ is the IV for SHA-512/t.

For $i = 0$ to 7
{
    $H_i^{(0)''} = H_i^{(0)'} \oplus \text{a5a5a5a5a5a5a5a5}$ (in hex).
}

$H^{(0)}$ = SHA-512 ("SHA-512/t") using $H^{(0)''}$ as the IV, where t is the specific truncation value.

(end.)

SHA-512/224 ($t = 224$) and SHA-512/256 ($t = 256$) are **approved** hash algorithms. Other SHA-512/t hash algorithms with different t values may be specified in [SP 800-107] in the future as the need arises. Below are the IVs for SHA-512/224 and SHA-512/256.

5.3.6.1   SHA-512/224

For SHA-512/224, the initial hash value, $H^{(0)}$, shall consist of the following eight 64-bit words, in hex:

$$H_0^{(0)} = \text{8C3D37C819544DA2}$$
$$H_1^{(0)} = \text{73E1996689DCD4D6}$$
$$H_2^{(0)} = \text{1DFAB7AE32FF9C82}$$
$$H_3^{(0)} = \text{679DD514582F9FCF}$$
$$H_4^{(0)} = \text{0F6D2B697BD44DA8}$$
$$H_5^{(0)} = \text{77E36F7304C48942}$$
$$H_6^{(0)} = \text{3F9D85A86A1D36C8}$$
$$H_7^{(0)} = \text{1112E6AD91D692A1}$$

These words were obtained by executing the *SHA-512/t IV Generation Function* with $t = 224$.

5.3.6.2   SHA-512/256

For SHA-512/256, the initial hash value, $H^{(0)}$, shall consist of the following eight 64-bit words, in hex:

$$H_0^{(0)} = \text{22312194FC2BF72C}$$
$$H_1^{(0)} = \text{9F555FA3C84C64C2}$$
$$H_2^{(0)} = \text{2393B86B6F53B151}$$
$$H_3^{(0)} = \text{963877195940EABD}$$
$$H_4^{(0)} = \text{96283EE2A88EFFE3}$$
$$H_5^{(0)} = \text{BE5E1E2553863992}$$
$$H_6^{(0)} = \text{2B0199FC2C85B8AA}$$
$$H_7^{(0)} = \text{0EB72DDC81C52CA2}$$

These words were obtained by executing the *SHA-512/t IV Generation Function* with $t = 256$.

6. SECURE HASH ALGORITHMS

In the following sections, the hash algorithms are not described in ascending order of size. SHA-256 is described before SHA-224 because the specification for SHA-224 is identical to SHA-256, except that different initial hash values are used, and the final hash value is truncated to 224 bits for SHA-224. The same is true for SHA-512, SHA-384, SHA-512/224 and SHA-512/256, except that the final hash value is truncated to 224 bits for SHA-512/224, 256 bits for SHA-512/256 or 384 bits for SHA-384.

For each of the secure hash algorithms, there may exist alternate computation methods that yield identical results; one example is the alternative SHA-1 computation described in Sec. 6.1.3. Such alternate methods may be implemented in conformance to this standard.

6.1   SHA-1

SHA-1 may be used to hash a message, M, having a length of ℓ bits, where $0 \le \ell < 2^{64}$. The algorithm uses 1) a message schedule of eighty 32-bit words, 2) five working variables of 32 bits each, and 3) a hash value of five 32-bit words. The final result of SHA-1 is a 160-bit message digest.

The words of the message schedule are labeled W_0, W_1,..., W_{79}. The five working variables are labeled a, b, c, d, and e. The words of the hash value are labeled $H_0^{(i)}, H_1^{(i)},..., H_4^{(i)}$, which will hold the initial hash value, $H^{(0)}$, replaced by each successive intermediate hash value (after each message block is processed), $H^{(i)}$, and ending with the final hash value, $H^{(N)}$. SHA-1 also uses a single temporary word, T.

6.1.1   SHA-1 Preprocessing

1. Set the initial hash value, $H^{(0)}$, as specified in Sec. 5.3.1.

2. The message is padded and parsed as specified in Section 5.

6.1.2   SHA-1 Hash Computation

The SHA-1 hash computation uses functions and constants previously defined in Sec. 4.1.1 and Sec. 4.2.1, respectively. Addition (+) is performed modulo 2^{32}.

Each message block, $M^{(1)}$, $M^{(2)}$, ..., $M^{(N)}$, is processed in order, using the following steps:

For $i=1$ to N:

{

    1. Prepare the message schedule, $\{W_t\}$:

$$W_t = \begin{cases} M_t^{(i)} & 0 \le t \le 15 \\ \\ ROTL^1(W_{t-3} \oplus W_{t-8} \oplus W_{t-14} \oplus W_{t-16}) & 16 \le t \le 79 \end{cases}$$

    2. Initialize the five working variables, a, b, c, d, and e, with the $(i-1)^{st}$ hash value:

$$a = H_0^{(i-1)}$$
$$b = H_1^{(i-1)}$$
$$c = H_2^{(i-1)}$$
$$d = H_3^{(i-1)}$$
$$e = H_4^{(i-1)}$$

    3. For $t=0$ to 79:

    {

$$T = ROTL^5(a) + f_t(b,c,d) + e + K_t + W_t$$
$$e = d$$
$$d = c$$
$$c = ROTL^{30}(b)$$
$$b = a$$
$$a = T$$

    }

    4. Compute the ith intermediate hash value $H^{(i)}$:

$$H_0^{(i)} = a + H_0^{(i-1)}$$
$$H_1^{(i)} = b + H_1^{(i-1)}$$
$$H_2^{(i)} = c + H_2^{(i-1)}$$
$$H_3^{(i)} = d + H_3^{(i-1)}$$
$$H_4^{(i)} = e + H_4^{(i-1)}$$

}

19

After repeating steps one through four a total of N times (i.e., after processing $M^{(N)}$), the resulting 160-bit message digest of the message, M, is

$$H_0^{(N)} \| H_1^{(N)} \| H_2^{(N)} \| H_3^{(N)} \| H_4^{(N)}$$

6.1.3   Alternate Method for Computing a SHA-1 Message Digest

The SHA-1 hash computation method described in Sec. 6.1.2 assumes that the message schedule W_0, W_1,..., W_{79} is implemented as an array of eighty 32-bit words. This is efficient from the standpoint of the minimization of execution time, since the addresses of W_{t-3},..., W_{t-16} in step (2) of Sec. 6.1.2 are easily computed.

However, if memory is limited, an alternative is to regard $\{W_t\}$ as a circular queue that may be implemented using an array of sixteen 32-bit words, W_0, W_1,..., W_{15}. The alternate method that is described in this section yields the same message digest as the SHA-1 computation method described in Sec. 6.1.2. Although this alternate method saves sixty-four 32-bit words of storage, it is likely to lengthen the execution time due to the increased complexity of the address computations for the $\{W_t\}$ in step (3).

For this alternate SHA-1 method, let $MASK$=0000000f (in hex). As in Sec. 6.1.1, addition is performed modulo 2^{32}. Assuming that the preprocessing as described in Sec. 6.1.1 has been performed, the processing of $M^{(i)}$ is as follows:

For i=1 to N:
{
1. For t=0 to 15:
    {
    $$W_t = M_t^{(i)}$$
    }

2. Initialize the five working variables, a, b, c, d, and e, with the $(i\text{-}1)^{st}$ hash value:

    $$a = H_0^{(i-1)}$$
    $$b = H_1^{(i-1)}$$
    $$c = H_2^{(i-1)}$$
    $$d = H_3^{(i-1)}$$
    $$e = H_4^{(i-1)}$$

3. For t=0 to 79:
    {
    $$s = t \wedge MASK$$

If $t \geq 16$ then
{
$$W_s = ROTL^1(W_{(s+13) \wedge MASK} \oplus W_{(s+8) \wedge MASK} \oplus W_{(s+2) \wedge MASK} \oplus W_s)$$
}

$$T = ROTL^5(a) + f_t(b,c,d) + e + K_t + W_s$$
$$e = d$$
$$d = c$$
$$c = ROTL^{30}(b)$$
$$b = a$$
$$a = T$$
}

4. Compute the ith intermediate hash value $H^{(i)}$:

$$H_0^{(i)} = a + H_0^{(i-1)}$$
$$H_1^{(i)} = b + H_1^{(i-1)}$$
$$H_2^{(i)} = c + H_2^{(i-1)}$$
$$H_3^{(i)} = d + H_3^{(i-1)}$$
$$H_4^{(i)} = e + H_4^{(i-1)}$$

}

After repeating steps one through four a total of N times (i.e., after processing $M^{(N)}$), the resulting 160-bit message digest of the message, M, is

$$H_0^{(N)} \| H_1^{(N)} \| H_2^{(N)} \| H_3^{(N)} \| H_4^{(N)}$$

6.2   SHA-256

SHA-256 may be used to hash a message, M, having a length of ℓ bits, where $0 \leq \ell < 2^{64}$. The algorithm uses 1) a message schedule of sixty-four 32-bit words, 2) eight working variables of 32 bits each, and 3) a hash value of eight 32-bit words. The final result of SHA-256 is a 256-bit message digest.

The words of the message schedule are labeled W_0, W_1,..., W_{63}. The eight working variables are labeled a, b, c, d, e, f, g, and h. The words of the hash value are labeled $H_0^{(i)}, H_1^{(i)},..., H_7^{(i)}$, which will hold the initial hash value, $H^{(0)}$, replaced by each successive intermediate hash value

21

(after each message block is processed), $H^{(i)}$, and ending with the final hash value, $H^{(N)}$. SHA-256 also uses two temporary words, T_1 and T_2.

6.2.1 SHA-256 Preprocessing

1. Set the initial hash value, $H^{(0)}$, as specified in Sec. 5.3.3.

2. The message is padded and parsed as specified in Section 5.

6.2.2 SHA-256 Hash Computation

The SHA-256 hash computation uses functions and constants previously defined in Sec. 4.1.2 and Sec. 4.2.2, respectively. Addition (+) is performed modulo 2^{32}.

Each message block, $M^{(1)}$, $M^{(2)}$, …, $M^{(N)}$, is processed in order, using the following steps:

For i=1 to N:
{

1. Prepare the message schedule, $\{W_t\}$:

$$
W_t = \begin{cases} M_t^{(i)} & 0 \le t \le 15 \\[2mm] \sigma_1^{\{256\}}(W_{t-2}) + W_{t-7} + \sigma_0^{\{256\}}(W_{t-15}) + W_{t-16} & 16 \le t \le 63 \end{cases}
$$

2. Initialize the eight working variables, a, b, c, d, e, f, g, and h, with the $(i\text{-}1)^{\text{st}}$ hash value:

$$a = H_0^{(i-1)}$$
$$b = H_1^{(i-1)}$$
$$c = H_2^{(i-1)}$$
$$d = H_3^{(i-1)}$$
$$e = H_4^{(i-1)}$$
$$f - II_5^{(i-1)}$$
$$g = H_6^{(i-1)}$$
$$h = H_7^{(i-1)}$$

22

3. For $t=0$ to 63:
{

$$T_1 = h + \sum_{1}^{\{256\}}(e) + Ch(e,f,g) + K_t^{\{256\}} + W_t$$

$$T_2 = \sum_{0}^{\{256\}}(a) + Maj(a,b,c)$$

$$h = g$$

$$g = f$$

$$f = e$$

$$e = d + T_1$$

$$d = c$$

$$c = b$$

$$b = a$$

$$a = T_1 + T_2$$

}

4. Compute the ith intermediate hash value $H^{(i)}$:

$$H_0^{(i)} = a + H_0^{(i-1)}$$

$$H_1^{(i)} = b + H_1^{(i-1)}$$

$$H_2^{(i)} = c + H_2^{(i-1)}$$

$$H_3^{(i)} = d + H_3^{(i-1)}$$

$$H_4^{(i)} = e + H_4^{(i-1)}$$

$$H_5^{(i)} = f + H_5^{(i-1)}$$

$$H_6^{(i)} = g + H_6^{(i-1)}$$

$$H_7^{(i)} = h + H_7^{(i-1)}$$

}

After repeating steps one through four a total of N times (i.e., after processing $M^{(N)}$), the resulting 256-bit message digest of the message, M, is

$$H_0^{(N)} \| H_1^{(N)} \| H_2^{(N)} \| H_3^{(N)} \| H_4^{(N)} \| H_5^{(N)} \| H_6^{(N)} \| H_7^{(N)}$$

6.3   SHA-224

SHA-224 may be used to hash a message, M, having a length of ℓ bits, where $0 \le \ell < 2^{64}$. The function is defined in the exact same manner as SHA-256 (Section 6.2), with the following two exceptions:

1. The initial hash value, $H^{(0)}$, shall be set as specified in Sec. 5.3.2; and

2. The 224-bit message digest is obtained by truncating the final hash value, $H(N)$, to its left-most 224 bits:

$$H_0^{(N)} \Vert H_1^{(N)} \Vert H_2^{(N)} \Vert H_3^{(N)} \Vert H_4^{(N)} \Vert H_5^{(N)} \Vert H_6^{(N)}$$

6.4 SHA-512

SHA-512 may be used to hash a message, M, having a length of ℓ bits, where $0 \le \ell < 2^{128}$. The algorithm uses 1) a message schedule of eighty 64-bit words, 2) eight working variables of 64 bits each, and 3) a hash value of eight 64-bit words. The final result of SHA-512 is a 512-bit message digest.

The words of the message schedule are labeled W_0, W_1,..., W_{79}. The eight working variables are labeled a, b, c, d, e, f, g, and h. The words of the hash value are labeled $H_0^{(i)}, H_1^{(i)}, \ldots, H_7^{(i)}$, which will hold the initial hash value, $H^{(0)}$, replaced by each successive intermediate hash value (after each message block is processed), $H^{(i)}$, and ending with the final hash value, $H^{(N)}$. SHA-512 also uses two temporary words, T_1 and T_2.

6.4.1 SHA-512 Preprocessing

1. Set the initial hash value, $H^{(0)}$, as specified in Sec. 5.3.5.

2. The message is padded and parsed as specified in Section 5.

6.4.2 SHA-512 Hash Computation

The SHA-512 hash computation uses functions and constants previously defined in Sec. 4.1.3 and Sec. 4.2.3, respectively. Addition (+) is performed modulo 2^{64}.

Each message block, $M^{(1)}$, $M^{(2)}$, ..., $M^{(N)}$, is processed in order, using the following steps:

For i=1 to N:
{

1. Prepare the message schedule, $\{W_t\}$:

$$W_t = \begin{cases} M_t^{(i)} & 0 \le t \le 15 \\ \\ \sigma_1^{\{512\}}(W_{t-2}) + W_{t-7} + \sigma_0^{\{512\}}(W_{t-15}) + W_{t-16} & 16 \le t \le 79 \end{cases}$$

2. Initialize the eight working variables, a, b, c, d, e, f, g, and h, with the $(i\text{-}1)^{\text{st}}$ hash value:

$$a = H_0^{(i-1)}$$
$$b = H_1^{(i-1)}$$
$$c = H_2^{(i-1)}$$
$$d = H_3^{(i-1)}$$
$$e = H_4^{(i-1)}$$
$$f = H_5^{(i-1)}$$
$$g = H_6^{(i-1)}$$
$$h = H_7^{(i-1)}$$

3. For t=0 to 79:
   {
$$T_1 = h + \sum\nolimits_1^{\{512\}}(e) + Ch(e,f,g) + K_t^{\{512\}} + W_t$$
$$T_2 = \sum\nolimits_0^{\{512\}}(a) + Maj(a,b,c)$$
$$h = g$$
$$g = f$$
$$f = e$$
$$e = d + T_1$$
$$d = c$$
$$c = b$$
$$b = a$$
$$a = T_1 + T_2$$

   }

4. Compute the ith intermediate hash value $H^{(i)}$:

$$H_0^{(i)} = a + H_0^{(i-1)}$$
$$H_1^{(i)} = b + H_1^{(i-1)}$$
$$H_2^{(i)} = c + H_2^{(i-1)}$$
$$H_3^{(i)} = d + H_3^{(i-1)}$$
$$H_4^{(i)} = e + H_4^{(i-1)}$$
$$H_5^{(i)} = f + H_5^{(i-1)}$$
$$H_6^{(i)} = g + H_6^{(i-1)}$$
$$H_7^{(i)} = h + H_7^{(i-1)}$$

}

After repeating steps one through four a total of N times (i.e., after processing $M^{(N)}$), the resulting 512-bit message digest of the message, M, is

$$H_0^{(N)} \| H_1^{(N)} \| H_2^{(N)} \| H_3^{(N)} \| H_4^{(N)} \| H_5^{(N)} \| H_6^{(N)} \| H_7^{(N)}$$

6.5   SHA-384

SHA-384 may be used to hash a message, M, having a length of ℓ bits, where $0 \le \ell < 2^{128}$. The algorithm is defined in the exact same manner as SHA-512 (Sec. 6.4), with the following two exceptions:

1. The initial hash value, $H^{(0)}$, shall be set as specified in Sec. 5.3.4; and

2. The 384-bit message digest is obtained by truncating the final hash value, $H^{(N)}$, to its left-most 384 bits:

$$H_0^{(N)} \| H_1^{(N)} \| H_2^{(N)} \| H_3^{(N)} \| H_4^{(N)} \| H_5^{(N)}$$

6.6   SHA-512/224

SHA-512/224 may be used to hash a message, M, having a length of ℓ bits, where $0 \le \ell < 2^{128}$. The algorithm is defined in the exact same manner as SHA-512 (Sec. 6.4), with the following two exceptions:

1. The initial hash value, $H^{(0)}$, shall be set as specified in Sec. 5.3.6.1; and

2. The 224-bit message digest is obtained by truncating the final hash value, $H^{(N)}$, to its left-most 224 bits.

6.7   SHA-512/256

SHA-512/256 may be used to hash a message, M, having a length of ℓ bits, where $0 \le \ell < 2^{128}$. The algorithm is defined in the exact same manner as SHA-512 (Sec. 6.4), with the following two exceptions:

1. The initial hash value, $H^{(0)}$, shall be set as specified in Sec. 5.3.6.2; and

2. The 256-bit message digest is obtained by truncating the final hash value, $H^{(N)}$, to its left-most 256 bits.

7. TRUNCATION OF A MESSAGE DIGEST

Some application may require a hash function with a message digest length different than those provided by the hash functions in this Standard. In such cases, a truncated message digest may be used, whereby a hash function with a larger message digest length is applied to the data to be hashed, and the resulting message digest is truncated by selecting an appropriate number of the leftmost bits. For guidelines on choosing the length of the truncated message digest and information about its security implications for the cryptographic application that uses it, see SP 800-107 [SP 800-107].

APPENDIX A: Additional Information

A.1 Security of the Secure Hash Algorithms

The security of the five hash algorithms, SHA-1, SHA-224, SHA-256, SHA-384, SHA-512, SHA-512/224 and SHA-512/256 is discussed in [SP 800-107].

A.2 Implementation Notes

Examples of SHA-1, SHA-224, SHA-256, SHA-384, SHA-512, SHA-512/224 and SHA-512/256 are available at http://csrc.nist.gov/groups/ST/toolkit/examples.html.

A.3 Object Identifiers

Object identifiers (OIDs) for the SHA-1, SHA-224, SHA-256, SHA-384, SHA-512, SHA-512/224 and SHA-512/256 algorithms are posted at http://csrc.nist.gov/groups/ST/crypto_apps_infra/csor/algorithms.html.

APPENDIX B: REFERENCES

[FIPS 180-3]   NIST, Federal Information Processing Standards Publication 180-3, *Secure Hash Standards (SHS)*, October 2008.

[SP 800-57]   NIST Special Publication (SP) 800-57, Part 1, *Recommendation for Key Management: General*, (Draft) May 2011.

[SP 800-107]   NIST Special Publication (SP) 800-107, *Recommendation for Applications Using Approved Hash Algorithms*, (Revised), (Draft) September 2011.

APPENDIX C: Technical Changes from FIPS 180-3

1. In FIPS 180-3, padding was inserted before hash computation begins. FIPS 140-4 removed this restriction. Padding can be inserted before hash computation begins or at any other time during the hash computation prior to processing the message block(s) containing the padding.

2. FIPS 180-4 adds two additional algorithms: SHA-512/224 and SHA-512/256 to the Standard and the method for determining the initial value for SHA-512/t for a given value of t.

www.ingramcontent.com/pod-product-compliance
Lightning Source LLC
Chambersburg PA
CBHW082106070326

40689CB00054B/4720